FLY HIGH

A Guide to Pilot and Air Cabin Crew Training

Rasheed Graham and Amanda Epe

FLY HIGH

A Guide to Pilot and Air Cabin Crew Training

by

Rasheed Graham

and

Amanda Epe

Blossom Books

LONDON

BLOSSOM BOOKS

First published in Great Britain

December 2020

Copyright © Rasheed Graham and Amanda Epe 2020

Rasheed Graham and Amanda Epe assert the moral right to be identified as the authors of this work.

A catalogue record of this book is available at the British Library

ISBN 9781838302504

All rights reserved. No part of this publication may be reproduced, stored in a retrieval system, or transmitted, in any form or by any means, electronic, mechanical, photocopying, recording or otherwise, without the prior permission of the publishers.

Dedication

Fly High is a book for young people who dare to challenge the norm and pursue their dreams. I dedicate this book to the supporters of #Rash2FlightSchool because without their generosity, I would not be where I am today.

Rasheed Graham

Fly High is for young people who aim to follow their dreams. I dedicate this work to the Jewel, my sister, who encourages me to go after mine.

Amanda Epe

'My soul is in the sky'

William Shakespeare

Table of contents

Dedication 5
Table of contents 7
PART ONE 9

Introduction to pilot training 10
Getting your foot through the door 17
Scholarships 22
Mentors 31
Integrated vs modular route 33
Should I go to university or straight into pilot training? 44
If I could go back in time what would I do differently? 47
PART TWO 53

Introduction to air cabin crew training 54
Reasons to fly for a living 59
Personal qualities for this role 62
    Cabin crew requisites 62
    Cabin crew responsibilities 63
Interviews and assessment 69
Cabin crew training 76

Safety and security 81
First aid kit 87
Airline terminology 97
In-flight assessment 105
Fly High 107
Acknowledgements 110

PART ONE

Introduction to pilot training

So, you want to become a pilot? Well, I can say you have made a superb choice.

While this book is only a guide to becoming a pilot, whether you want to fly as a private pilot for leisure or pursue a career as a commercial or military pilot, technically, there is no fixed way to achieve either, but the best route is the route that works best for **YOU**. Looking back, during my teens I wish I had found information that came from personal experience rather than a generic sales piece from a big company wanting to take your money and not answering the real questions. When I was at school, teachers and careers advisors did not tell me I could become a pilot, so if I can make the journey easier for the next generation of aviators, then why not?

So, what is the role of a pilot?

- **To fly passengers and cargo from one destination to another across the nation or the world.**

- **To ensure the safety of passengers, crew and aircraft.**

- **To check and inspect the aircraft and its controls for operational efficiency and safety before take-off.**

- To study and analyse the route and flight plans before take-off.

- To observe and check weather conditions.

- To keep in touch and communicate with air traffic control while piloting the aircraft.

- To conduct pre-flight checks on the navigation and operating systems.

- To calculate the fuel intake and load and fuel the aircraft accordingly.

- **To brief and maintain regular contact with the flight crew throughout the flight.**

- **To react appropriately to ensure the safety of passengers and crew during emergencies and adverse circumstances.**

Everyone's journey to becoming a pilot is different. When you speak to pilots or trainees, you will hear some similar stories, but the vast majority of people pursue different avenues to achieve the goal of flying planes. However, all pilots have the following five core skills in common.

1. Clear communication

2. Situational awareness

3. Team-working

4. Decisiveness and quick-thinking

5. Leadership

While I believe that any journey to becoming a pilot is about personal development, if you do not already possess these skills, you will learn and develop them with the help of this guide.

The first step is to ask yourself why you want to be a pilot? There are thousands of careers and hobbies that you can pursue, but what is the defining factor about becoming a pilot that resonates with you? While there is no right or wrong answer, I believe that this question is important before fastening your seatbelt and jetting off into a career in aviation. From the perspective of a trainee, being a pilot looks glamorous and, don't get me wrong, it is an amazing career and one I would not think twice about pursuing. However, there are aspects of the role that will push your limits, and there will be times throughout your training and career where you will face obstacles and ultimately ask yourself 'why?' This will be the defining moment that gets you through those tough times. I decided that I wanted to be a pilot at three or four years old, and what was the deciding factor for me? I have no idea. Some may say it was fate, but I put it down to the 'aviation bug'. No one in my family is a pilot or works in aviation, so I believe it is something I was simply destined to do. I love flying, and I love the impact that flying has on other people, whether it is watching the smile on someone's face as they return from their first flight or seeing families and friends reunite in the arrival's hall. Whatever the occasion, I simply enjoy helping others while doing something I love.

Getting your foot through the door

Now for the serious stuff. Unfortunately, getting into flying is inherently expensive and becoming a pilot is a big investment. Do not let this put you off as I have been in the position where you think you can't afford the training costs, but in this instance, you will need sheer determination and resilience.

Research is paramount to ensure you are getting the most for your money while getting the most out of your training. Therefore, it is wise that you meet the medical requirements to be a pilot by completing a medical by an aeromedical examiner; the last thing you want to do is invest a large sum of money into flying only to find out that you are not fit to fly. For those who want to fly for leisure, you will need to meet the medical requirements for a light aircraft pilot licence (LAPL) or a Class 2 medical. To pursue the commercial route, you will need to meet the requirements of a Class 1 medical, which is more stringent. However, if you do not meet the medical requirements of Class 1, you may still be able to pass a Class 2 or LAPL medical.

Once you have been issued with your shiny new LAPL, Class 2 or 1 medical, you can start learning to fly. At this point, there are two available licences to train towards:

1. **Light aircraft pilot licence (LAPL)**
2. **Private pilot licence (PPL)**

Both licences allow an individual to act as a pilot-in-command of a single-engine light aircraft. However, you are unable to receive remuneration. Depending on your aspirations, this will determine what licence you wish to pursue. A LAPL is designed for individuals who would like to fly recreationally and requires a minimum of 30 hours flight time and passes in nine theory exams, including:

- **Principles of flight**
- **Meteorology**

- Aircraft general knowledge
- Navigation
- Air law
- Operational procedures
- Human performance
- Flight planning
- Performance and communications

A PPL is for those who want to fly recreationally but may have the aspiration to pursue a commercial pilot's licence (CPL) in the future. This licence requires a minimum of 45 hours flight time and passes in the nine exams listed above. Unfortunately, it is not possible to train for a commercial pilot licence with a LAPL, but you can upgrade your LAPL to a PPL with further training.

The timescales to complete each licence depends on a wide range of factors, including the student's ability, personal life, weather, instructor/aircraft availability, among others. If you plan to fly every other weekend this could take from 1–1.5 years to complete, whereas if you have the time to embark on an intensive course and all the stars align, you could complete your licence within 5–6 weeks.

Scholarships

There are ways to significantly cut down the cost of pilot training, some of which I have used to my advantage. Various organisations provide scholarships for those who want to start flying and those currently in training. These scholarships are worth their weight in gold because they give applicants who may not have the means to pay for flying lessons upfront the opportunity to start training.

I have been lucky enough to be awarded five scholarships in my journey to becoming a pilot. I have been awarded two gliding scholarships, which allowed me to learn to fly a glider. This was a thoroughly enjoyable experience as gliding cements the foundation of all the skills you will learn as a pilot. I would recommend gliding to anyone who wants to start flying as it is a great way to figure out if flying is for you, and it is considerably cheaper than powered flying as some gliding clubs charge as little as £17 to get airborne.

I was then awarded a 12-hour powered flying scholarship, which allowed me to complete 12 hours flying as part of the PPL syllabus. During the course, I completed my first solo flight in a powered aircraft and sat my first PPL exam. Your first solo is the highlight of any student pilot's career, and it marks the accumulation of the core fundamental skills you have learnt and developed at this stage of the course. For me, it was an experience that I have never forgotten because your first solo is the point where your instructor trusts you to fly an aircraft by yourself!

I remember flying a circuit at Dundee airport; I looked over at my instructor's seat and realised he wasn't there – I was actually flying the aircraft all by myself. Luckily, the year after my first powered flying scholarship I was awarded the best scholar from my cohort, and I was able to fly a further 30 hours and sit the remaining eight PPL exams. This allowed me to complete my LAPL so I could act as pilot-in-command of a single-engine light aircraft. I cannot stress the importance of applying for scholarships; without these opportunities, I do not think I would be where I am today. I have come across several aspiring pilots who are confused by the number of scholarships that I have been awarded, but the truth is, I was simply looking in the right places.

Scholarships are very competitive, and thousands of individuals apply for a limited number of places each year. Therefore, it is paramount that your applications stand out. This is an opportunity to sell yourself, really prove why you want to become a pilot and why a sponsor should fund you to achieve this. I was rejected for scholarships for two years before being awarded my first flying scholarship, so don't be disheartened if you're not successful on your first attempt because this is a journey in which you'll face many setbacks and this will be a testament to how you bounce back, so keep on applying. The best advice I can give to anyone applying for scholarships is to have a 'master application', which is a general personal statement that can be tailored to the specific organisation you are applying to.

These are the key areas you should be thinking of when you are writing your personal statements for scholarships:

1. **Why should you be awarded a scholarship?**

2. **What are your specific career aims?**

3. **Hobbies and interests**

4. **Sporting achievements**

5. **Work experience**

6. **Charity work**

The aim is to provide real-life examples in these areas while demonstrating the core skills of a pilot.

There are other ways to get into flying, especially from a young age. The Air Cadets is a great stepping stone to becoming a pilot. The cadets provide you with copious life skills that are useful both as a pilot and in other fields. However, they also provide flying experience, which is invaluable as it relieves you of the financial cost. I started in the Air Cadets, and I am so glad I joined; the flying instruction is second to none as you get to fly with military and airline pilots. You gain so many skills and knowledge at an early stage in your life that you will go on to talk about in your career.

Another hidden gem is the University Air Squadron. This is where certain UK universities have a squadron associated with the reserve Royal Air Force. I studied at Loughborough University, and I was lucky enough to get a place as an Officer Cadet at East Midlands University Air Squadron (UAS) in my first year. Unfortunately, the UAS system does not recruit from all universities across the country so you will need to attend an associated university to be able to apply. My time on the UAS gave me an exceptional university experience, and if I had not been accepted into the squadron, I probably would not have gone to university. The main attraction of the UAS is the flying, and by the time I had finished, I had logged over 50 hours in the Grob Tutor T1. I cannot stress how valuable this was to my development as a relatively junior pilot. My most notable moment during my time with the UAS was my first solo flight, which was even more surreal because I was sent up by the Queen's former pilot!

Mentors

The pilot community is generally quite small and is filled with people who share the same passion. In the early stages, it can be quite difficult to navigate the copious amounts of information that you may come across in your research, and one thing I can say is that you should not do it alone. This is where a mentor comes in. I describe a mentor as a 'cheat code' to the industry because they have an abundance of experience in the career you are trying to get into and can provide you with personal anecdotes, which are more valuable than any information you will find online. I had a mentor who was a pilot from the age of 17, and they guided me and gave me advice on the steps I should take to get into flying. There is no time limit on when you should get a mentor; some say you should start earlier or you could start later, the bottom line is you should have one. Nowadays, you can find experienced pilots on social media who are within reach and willing to help people who are in the same position they were once in, so it is a no-brainer to use their expertise to your advantage.

Integrated vs modular route

Once you have a new shiny licence or some flying hours under your belt and you want to take this flying malarky to the next level, what's next? There are two routes to becoming a commercial pilot: integrated and modular.

The most common route taken by aspiring pilots is the integrated route. This is an intensive course offered by big flying schools across the world. They are approximately 14-18 months in duration, and you complete the course on a residential basis where you live and learn at your chosen flight training organisation. On the other hand, the modular course is tailored to the individual, whereby the student can break the course down into modules and complete their flying training in stages.

There are ongoing debates about the best route to take as an aspiring pilot. While both routes have their pros and cons, your final decision ultimately comes down to what YOU want and your financial situation. I was fortunate to embark on the integrated route at Flight Training Europe in Jerez, Spain. For me, this was the best possible option as all the facilities I needed were in one place. I studied and lived in a full-board campus, which meant I didn't have to work, cook or clean! This allowed me to complete the necessary 250 hours of flying and fully focus on the 14 Air Transport Pilot Licence (ATPL) exams, which are compulsory exams that you must pass to get your licence. The modules included:

- **Principles of flight**
- **General navigation**
- **Meteorology**
- **Aircraft general knowledge**
- **Instruments**
- **Radio navigation**
- **Flight planning**
- **Mass and balance**
- **Air law**
- **Human performance**
- **Operational procedures**

- **VFR/IFR communications and aircraft performance**

I was on the course with other cadets, so we could learn from each other and vice versa. This was invaluable to me because I found ground school particularly challenging, so I was able to draw upon the expertise of other cadets in my class when I needed to. However, attending an integrated school comes with significant financial implications, and to attend some of the biggest schools in Europe can incur costs of up to £120,000 without the guarantee of a job at the end of your training. Therefore, it is paramount that you do plenty of research by attending open days for different schools, speaking to present and past students and visiting careers fairs so you can ensure that you are choosing a school that meets all of your requirements. From my experience of training on an integrated course, I would not take a loan out against property if I had the means to as the risk is high and you are committed to finishing the course; in the unlikely situation that you fail to complete the course, you would be left without a licence and in a mountain of debt. This is an amazing career but not worth the stress of getting into crippling debt or risking your parents' property.

It is advantageous but not compulsory to train at an integrated school with the backing of an airline, which ensures that you have a secure job at the airline after you graduate. This puts less pressure on you during training as all you must do is complete the course with the best possible marks. I was lucky enough to be selected for a fully sponsored Future Pilots Programme with a leading European airline, so I went into training knowing that I would be graduating into the right-hand seat of an Airbus 320/321.

The second route is the modular route, which requires you to possess a PPL before commencing. A student must complete the ATPL course in blocks at a pace that suits them, which can take anywhere between 1.5

and 3 years. This route is beneficial as it allows the individual to maintain a job while completing their training. The modular route is significantly cheaper than the integrated route as the student is not tied to any one Flight Training Organisation and can shop around at smaller organisations at a cheaper cost. Furthermore, the aviation industry is volatile and as I write, the industry is currently faced with its worst-ever disaster with the coronavirus pandemic severely reducing air travel. Therefore, the likelihood of a newly qualified commercial pilot landing a job with an airline is relatively slim but not entirely impossible. In the current climate, it would be advantageous for aspiring pilots to pursue the modular route as you will have more control over how and when you complete your training, and you would qualify as a commercial pilot when the industry begins to recover as opposed to qualifying in a climate where there are thousands of unemployed pilots across the world and gaining your first job will be competitive.

The downside to the modular route is continuity. Taking the integrated route allows you to complete the course in one go; however, with the modular route, the flow of training is inconsistent and there may be gaps. Personally, I preferred the continuity, but for others, the ability to cut down costs or work around a training schedule may be more favourable.

For those who are considering the modular route, I would recommend sitting an aptitude test after completing your PPL. This test measures the natural skills of an individual through various test formats and will determine your suitability to become a commercial pilot. As previously mentioned, becoming a pilot is a big investment, so you want to ensure you are suitable for the role before commencing your training. Moreover, if you sit an aptitude test and do not meet the required standard, do not be disheartened because it does not mean you cannot be a pilot, it simply highlights the areas you need to work on to become more suitable for the job. There are plenty of websites offering aptitude tests to help you prepare, but from experience, I believe that being comfortable with mental arithmetic is important as you need to problem-solve quickly and correctly during pilot training and in the theory phase of the course. If maths isn't your speciality, don't worry, I wasn't the best at maths, but I did just fine on the aptitude test and during the course; it will come with practice.

Whatever route you take in terms of your training, the outcome is the same. At the end of your integrated or modular training, you will be awarded an ATPL, which will allow you to start applying for your first flying job.

Should I go to university or straight into pilot training?

While a university degree is not a requirement for becoming a pilot, there are many benefits of going to university. Once again, this is up to personal preference, but ultimately, you need to think about why you should or should not go to university. First, a university degree may serve as a backup option in case you don't make it as a pilot for whatever reason. A degree is a good plan B where you could transition into another career path if you cannot secure a job as a pilot immediately. Going to university is also a great time for personal development, especially for those who are fresh out of college/sixth form because this is the perfect time to gain some life experience in terms of living away from home, handling personal finances, meeting new people and being independent. Additionally, the university experience offers valuable extracurricular activities, such as societies, sports teams and positions of responsibility, which will help form you into a well-rounded asset for any flying school or airline. I believe that this is advantageous to your experience during pilot training and beyond as you will be accustomed the lifestyle of a student on a higher education course, which will assist you in adjusting to the steep learning curve of the pilot training system.

On the other hand, if you think university is not for you, explore the option of going to work and even combine this with travelling. My advice to those leaving college/sixth form is to gain a wealth of experience before embarking on your training. As a commercial pilot, you will potentially have a career that spans over forty years so it works well in your favour to take part in opportunities that will develop you as an individual and make you a well-rounded character attractive to any airline or flying job.

If I could go back in time what would I do differently?

The best advice I can give to any aspiring pilot is to enjoy the journey. One of the mistakes I made growing up is that I became so fixated on becoming a pilot that I turned down other valuable opportunities. For example, in high school, I had the opportunity to fundraise and travel to Swaziland to build a classroom in a school during the summer holidays. At the same time, I was waiting to hear if I was successful in getting a gliding scholarship with the Air Cadets, so I made a very impulsive decision and dropped out of the programme in the hope that it would not clash with my scholarship. Unfortunately, I did not get a scholarship and I missed the opportunity to travel to Swaziland. In hindsight, I should have taken every opportunity available to me even if they were not aviation-related because I would have been building a wealth of experience in different areas, which is important when you're applying for your first scholarship, sponsorship or even your first job.

Do what you enjoy and what makes you happy. I say this because in my teenage years especially, I was under the impression that I needed to be a whizz at physics and maths to be a pilot. While they are important subjects, it is not mandatory to be an A* student. In my first year of A-levels, I studied maths, physics and biology because I thought these were ideal subjects for someone pursuing a career as a pilot, which couldn't be further from the truth. I probably picked the worst subjects as I ended up finishing my first year with E, U, U. As you can imagine, I was devastated, but I learned that I needed to do more of what I enjoyed, so I retook my first year of sixth form studying different subjects and I ended up with good grades.

Do not be afraid to fail. Falling short of your desired objective doesn't mean you will never get there; it simply means you have to go back to the drawing board to see where you went wrong and put a plan of action in place to fix it. If I had not received poor results in the sixth form, I would not have had the opportunity to experience failure until later in life, perhaps where it mattered the most. Throughout your training, you will be thrown in the deep end and be expected to adapt very quickly, which might not work out the way you want it to, so having the ability to reflect, be aware of your strengths and weaknesses and be able to problem-solve is paramount to succeeding both through your training and your career as a pilot.

Do not be scared to ask for help. Let's be honest, we are all human and we cannot figure everything out for ourselves all the time, so it is important to learn to ask for help when it is needed. During your training, you will come across students of varying ability and although it looks like everyone has it together all of the time, the reality is, we are all just as lost as each other. During ground school, I was in a class of 16 sponsored airline cadets of which most were university graduates, even some doctors, so I felt the need to always keep up with the crowd, and I am sure that others felt the same. My point is, do not suffer in silence because you are not helping yourself, and be aware that there is always someone out there to help you.

I hope this guide has been useful so far and made you aware of the various options that are available to you. Remember that this is a marathon, not a race, and hopefully, I will see you on a flight deck at some point in the future.

PART TWO

Introduction to air cabin crew training

Why write *A Guide to Air Cabin Crew Training*? It's for you, and that is the simple answer. After penning my debut memoir, *A Fly Girl: Travel Tales*, I listened to the responses of readers and read reviews of the book. Whilst many people enjoyed reading about my travel experiences when working for an airline, some wanted to gain more insight into my flight experiences and learn more about the industry, including the training programme. Readers wanted me to write more and kept asking when the next edition was coming out.

My intention in writing *A Fly Girl* was to share my stories with the public for self-empowerment, reader entertainment and enlightenment about the ins and outs of cabin crew lifestyle and travel experiences. *A Guide to Air Cabin Crew Training* is for those who want the introductory knowledge, skills and training needed to work as cabin crew and who have an interest in aviation careers. It seemed timely to write this book now because I recently met Rasheed Graham who has long-term ambitions to encourage young people to step into aviation. In my career in education, I also encourage children and young people to believe in their dreams and be adventurous, so writing this book in collaboration with Rasheed would serve as a tool to guide and encourage young people in this field.

OK, my other reason is that I love writing! It allows me to tell stories and encourage people to read. Rather than write solely educational lessons on cabin crew training, I thought it would be far more interesting to share my experiences and feelings during my training for a more in-depth understanding of what it is like. I've also included some simple exercises for readers to do.

Hopefully, you enjoy writing as well. Perhaps your future will involve a lot of travel, and if you pursue an aviation career, you may want to write notes about your journeys. Pilots are always writing notes and jotting things in their logbooks about their flights. As cabin crew staff, you have to write notes and reports in the crew logbook, and some cabin crew write in journals for their personal benefit. So, I have combined my stories with ideas for you to write reflectively about your thoughts and intentions about a job as a flight attendant.

This guide is written from my experiences of training and incorporates research from the industry today. It is not often that school pupils or students get the opportunity to meet people from the industry they desire to work in. Some schools provide work experience weeks or taster days and invite key speakers to a school assembly. Another place for accessing information is through careers guidance. This book provides both key speakers' perspectives from the stories they tell and career guidance.

It's time to fasten your seat belt as we enter the simulator and travel through the training rooms. Let's go.

Reasons to fly for a living

Why do you want to fly? You will get a shock if you believe that you want to travel the world easily at low cost. Being a cabin crew member means you are flying for work, not pleasure! Many of us get it twisted. I wanted to travel the world to be a travel writer, and finding work as a flight attendant was a stepping stone to achieving this goal or so I thought. I found out that it wasn't a stepping stone, it was more like climbing over rocks. The work is not as glamorous as it may appear with the uniform and jet-set life. So, I will forewarn you by describing what the work entails and you can find out if you are the right fit. Working as cabin crew trains you to be multi-skilled in areas such as hospitality, security, counselling, caring, retail and many more service areas. You're going to need mental and physical dexterity, so a little checklist of personal qualities would be useful as you delve into your training guide.

WHY FLY?   **AVIATION**
IS THIS JOB FOR ME?   **KNOWLEDGE TEST:**

FLYING AND APPLYING

Write an expository paragraph on this subject.

What is the best place you've visited?
What do you know about flying, it could be about an airline's history,
chronicles in aviation or your understanding of altitude?
Give five reasons why you want to fly for a living.

Personal qualities for this role

Various personality types are suited to working as cabin crew; many are outgoing, extroverted and lively but all are people-orientated. A job advertisement I responded to were recruiting people with a creative flair, something I didn't know was a necessary skill for a flight attendant. However, there are so many skills one can bring to this industry, and I've listed what airline industries are looking for below.

Cabin crew requisites

- **Experience as previous cabin crew (some airlines require this)**

- Fluency in English

- Additional languages

- Cabin crew certificate and/or Travel and Tourism Studies

- Customer service experience

- Communication skills

Cabin crew responsibilities

- Welcome and steward passengers, also welcome in another language.

- Assist passengers and support those needing assistance to their seats

- **Answer all questions and queries**

- **Ensure customer satisfaction**

- **Check the safety of the aircraft before passengers embark**

- **Check the safety of the cabin before take-off**

- **Present safety demonstrations**

- **Monitor the cabin from boarding through to disembarking**

- Take orders and serve beverages and set meals.

- Sell duty-free products

- Assist passengers during emergency landings

- Assist in medical emergencies

- Special care and attention to the elderly, disabled and special needs passengers.

- Solve passenger disputes

- **Restrain passengers breaking airline regulations**

- **IT skills for on the aircraft and Microsoft knowledge**

Find three examples for each area of your life and/or work experience that stands out using the above cabin crew requisites and responsibilities. Think of these points as if asked about them in an interview scenario.

Communication skills

1

2

3

Customer service skills

1

2

3

Relevant courses

1

2

3

Emergencies

1

2

3

Care work experience

1

2

3

Interviews and assessment

The day you receive notification that you have been shortlisted for an interview is a day for rejoicing because being seen by the recruitment department shows great potential. Thousands of people apply hoping for a taste of the sky life, but only a handful are selected. Therefore, it is necessary to make sure your application is a cut above the rest.

Your application should be drafted first, then re-written. Take a break and then re-read it, adding and/or deleting parts as appropriate. It may be useful to show it to someone who works in human resources or a recruitment expert, but failing this, a trusted friend or family member could also point out some of the skills that they recognise in you that need to be added to your application.

Being invited for an interview is part of a long process to gain an employment contract as a flight attendant. Just like your application form, you will have to stand out on the day as many airlines have mass recruitment days where it is a process of elimination from the morning until the end of the day. Therefore, you should not rest on your laurels when you've been shortlisted for an interview.

I mastered several flight attendant application forms and had been shortlisted for several interviews but was unsuccessful in all of them. I was usually sent home by the end of the morning session. However, one particular time I made it through to the afternoon, and I felt elated. It was an interview for a major airline, and I was feeling victorious, getting comfortable after lunch and thinking about what the afternoon tasks were going to be. Suddenly, my name was called, and I was asked to have a chat with one of the staff. My heart sank when I was told to go home, but it was only after arriving at home that the outcome sank in. I felt like I had been fired; one moment I was confident that I had gotten through, and in an instant, it was over.

I tell this story because I want you to be prepared for the process; it is lengthy, challenging and you need endurance. If you really want this work, you will endure rejection time and time again as I did until I was finally successful sometime after I got over the rejection. Nevertheless, the real test is not being employed after the interview and assessment; it is the training programme, which is usually a six-week programme. Before we get into that though, I want you to reflect on the things that make you stand out so you are guaranteed to be called for an interview. If I were an employer and I was looking for the soft skills needed for this job – compassion, empathy and helpfulness – I would want to see these traits in the areas we have discussed. I'd also look out for someone's knowledge and experiences. Think about the work you have done within a community group to show your people skills. You may have gained particular knowledge in aircraft specifications; if so, you would make a standout candidate who is passionate about aviation.

Use the table to make notes about your knowledge, skills and experiences in the three areas of people, places and planes. It can be anything from the history of planes to technical information, places you have visited, the cultures you have experienced and the significant impact you have made on people. After these tasks, try to deliberately set out and practice interpersonal skills with strangers as you may need this for your assessment.

People	Places	Planes
1	1	1
2	2	2
3	3	3
4	4	4
5	5	5
6	6	6
7	7	7
8	8	8
9	9	9
10	10	10

Cabin crew training

You are almost ready to fly, hypothetically speaking. You have been successfully shortlisted, passed the assessments and interview and now the toughest work begins in training. It is like returning to school again; lessons range from food and hygiene to understanding global norms and cultures. For example, this would entail learning topics in the food technology curriculum, such as the correct temperature for specific food stored in a fridge or freezer. You would also learn about etiquette, especially when greeting people in terms of where it is acceptable or unacceptable to touch international passengers.

The first lesson that is a necessity is perseverance, and I cannot stress this enough. If you have ever watched TV shows like Alan Sugar's *The Apprentice*, you will get the picture of what cabin crew training is like. The camera is on you from the beginning of the day until you return home and take off your uniform. You are constantly being assessed and monitored to evaluate your behaviour and attitude in all situations.

During your interview psychometric testing was used for analysis, the same applies when in crew training you are put into different teams to work on group tasks. It is essential to have excellent team working skills as this is dependent on effectively working together to fulfil your service role. Ideally, you will be a flexible person who can adapt to working with different personality types, and that is why they have chosen you to become an employee. However, there will be days when your colleagues irritate you, perhaps even frustrate you, and my best advice is to remain calm and if there is a grievance, speak about it in a professional capacity. If you have come this far, you don't want to spoil your opportunities because of unruly disputes and believe me, you will encounter disputes all the time in the skies. The probability of having a flight with no passenger upsets is very slim, but you need to use your innate problem-solving skills when you see issues escalating. When you know what a typical day could be like, it is much easier to handle colleague confrontations; it is the first small hurdle.

As with *The Apprentice* and other competitive programmes, we often see the contestants' insecurity. This is similar in a training programme as participants are naturally nervous and anxious about passing the programme. This could lead to unhealthy competition as to who will get through, but there will probably be supportive people around you, and if you are fortunate, you could make trusted friends. In any case, you must persevere with friends or foes in your training community; you have to see the bigger picture of your dream to fly as this will get you through. Everything else is a small distraction. During my training, I became distracted by some negative vibrations that were felt and shown, yet I was also fortunate to have one friend in my training group and because I was so eager to fly, the negativity became insignificant. My best advice is to find a supportive learning bubble as you are all in this together.

The lives of cabin crew are consistently on the move, and this begins in training. The programme's intensity will prepare you to look after your wellbeing, to learn, work, rest and play.

Safety and security

The fundamental reason why cabin crew members are employed is for the safety and security of passengers. Even if there were no food, beverage or duty-free services on the flight, staff would still be on board to fulfil the legal requirements for air safety. It is good to know that people are still valued in this industry compared to others where people have been replaced by automated devices and voices. On an aircraft, a flight attendant is an important resource for the safety and comfort of the passenger's journey. For this reason, Safety and

Emergency Procedures (SEP) are key training components.

A flight attendant has to be a certain weight and height before being recruited, which is not related to aesthetics. To be in good health, your weight should be in line with your height, so your body mass index (BMI) is recorded as part of your initial assessment day. You need to be able to move and lift for long periods to perform your role. Height is crucial, as a flight attendant needs to be able to reach the overhead lockers to open and close them, and they must not exceed a certain height that they will have difficulty bending. Height restrictions are for the benefit of overall safety and the person's ability to do the work. Most airlines require their staff to be no shorter than 5ft 2in and no taller than 6ft 3in. In addition to height, having good eyesight is also important in carrying out cabin crew duties. Your eyesight is normally screened as part of your medical examination once you have passed the interview. Part of safety requires being alert and thinking on your feet so quick thinking is another skill in the long list of essentials.

Part of your training requires being in a flight simulator for the real-life experience of the practical side of the operation. One of the first tasks in my training was to turn the power-assisted aircraft doors from manual to automatic. How you perform this depends on the model of the aircraft. As part of your training, you do this several times to be fully confident and competent in an emergency. You also need to be prepared for jumping out and sliding down the escape slide.

Training also includes emergency landings and ditching, the landing in the event of a flight having to land in the water. Many airlines request that staff are good swimmers, and part of the training may include a day at a swimming pool to practice rescuing passengers. I am not a good swimmer, and I barely passed this part, so I would recommend improving your swimming ability just to be on the safe side.

Back on the ground, there will be trips to airport terminals to gain hands-on experience on actual planes and to learn where the emergency operational equipment is stowed. It is essential to know where to locate the plug in the passenger service unit (PSU) sockets when administering oxygen, where the fire safety equipment is located and how to use it. It is also mandatory to keep the captain safe and look after his/her wellbeing, so training covers emergency first aid in the cockpit too.

If you are fascinated by aircraft and want to know more to help you stand out as an applicant and help you in your training, it is advisable to visit aerodromes, simulators or use online technology to see how things work. Otherwise, do what you are doing now and read aviation books for more in-depth knowledge of aircraft.

My security training opened my eyes to the unexpected. It explored global and socio-political issues, war zones, espionage, detonators, self-defence training and restraining acts. Try to imagine the type of security needed to work as a flight attendant, especially in light of the COVID-19 pandemic because with cases of emergency evacuations prevalent, there could be all sorts of safety and emergency scenarios.

First aid kit

We've identified that the role of cabin crew is to ensure safety at all times. In addition to firefighting, first aid also needs to be administered should a passenger become ill or injured during the flight. Cabin crew are required to help passengers with basic first aid when alerted to someone in distress. Normally, cabin crew keep an eye on passengers when boarding and during a flight to ensure their safety. However, people are not always aware that they are ill, so it may not be the passenger themselves that calls cabin crew for help. If the passenger is travelling alone or seated next to a stranger, it could be another passenger who rings the bell. There could be a delay in accessing help if the stranger does not realise what is happening, or thinks that the passenger is displaying normal behaviour. It can also be difficult to know if the passenger is in a deep sleep or if they have passed out. Cabin crew must be alert for this at all times. Alarm bells are more likely when a passenger is having a fit, slumping or gasping for breath.

Medical scenarios on a flight come in a wide variety. Some passengers could have serious health conditions, and those with special medical conditions are listed for the crew to know who they are and where they are seated; in some cases, they are given special seating arrangements. Some medical emergencies could result from a fear of flying where the passenger has a panic attack or they could get scalded from hot water when being served a hot drink. Turbulent flights can also be a hazard; this is why the announcement for passengers to return to their seats and put their seat belts on is very serious as accidents can occur. During the flight, passengers can access the overhead lockers, but if they don't shut properly, cases and bags can fall from the locker during turbulence causing a head injury or concussion. Flight attendants are always looking for overhead lockers that aren't shut. Passengers can also become nauseous from overeating, excessive consumption of alcohol, food poisoning or allergies. There are extreme cases where people have had heart attacks, women have gone into labour and sadly, people have died.

When crew members are called for a medical emergency, they first have to make a patient assessment and take notes. Although they are trained to administer initial first aid, their knowledge in medical emergencies is limited, so the next procedure is for the captain to be notified if the medical issue is urgent. The cabin manager (or purser) then puts a call out to ask if there are any medical doctors, nurses or paramedics on board. If you have ever heard an announcement from the flight deck asking for a doctor, this is the standard protocol for addressing medical emergencies. The call for a health professional comes after assessing the severity of the issue and deciding whether medical intervention is necessary or not. Following an assessment from a medical professional, if they diagnose a serious health problem, the flight destination can be changed.

Flight diversion is an aviation legal requirement that can happen due to an emergency on board. The pilot, doctor and team of flight attendants work in close communication to monitor the patient, and the captain will relay information through the Aircraft Communications Addressing and Reporting System (ACARS). The flight can land at the nearest airport or a suitable aerodrome to transfer the passenger to ground emergency services.

During my training, I practised assessing ill passengers on a dummy, and we role-played with the rest of the trainees in the training room, simulator and on the aircraft. One of the striking things I noticed was that it was a tight space to work in, which reflected the real-world situation that if a passenger was taken ill, they would have to lie down in the aisle of the aircraft. We used the ABCs of first aid on scenarios, such as strokes and heart attacks.

- **Airway: check if the patient has an open airway**
- **Breathing: check if the patient is breathing**
- **Circulation: check to detect a heartbeat**

If there was no heartbeat, the patient was not breathing or had a blocked airway, we had to perform cardiopulmonary resuscitation (CPR).

As you would expect, the first aid kit is full of medical instruments and survival apparatus, such as oxygen tanks. An aircraft does not have the space capacity of a hospital so only the necessary items can be stored on the plane.

Cabin crew are trained to administer oxygen to passengers with breathing difficulties. The oxygen is carried in portable cylinders and the patient is fitted with a mask. Regulators alert the crew to how much of a dose is being given. As qualified cabin crew, the training permits you to use an automated external defibrillator should any heart-related emergency occur. Other items in the first aid kit are medication that cabin crew can prescribe and a physician's kit; this is only allowed to be administered by a licenced medical practitioner. However, part of cabin crew training is to learn the different parts of the kit and understand why are they are there and how it is used. I think you'll get ahead if you had a sneak preview of what is inside the kit. Some of the items in the kit include the following (sourced from the Civil Aviation Medical Association):

Medication	Equipment
• Epinephrine 1:1,000 • Injectable (inj) antihistamine • Dextrose 50% inj. 50 mL (or equivalent) • Nitroglycerin tablets or spray • Major analgesic, inj or oral • Sedative anticonvulsant, inj • Antiemetic, inj • Bronchial dilator inhaler • Atropine, inj • Corticosteroid, inj • Diuretic, inj • Medication for postpartum bleeding • Normal saline • Acetylsalicylic acid for oral use • Oral beta-blocker • Epinephrine 1:10,000	• Stethoscope • Sphygmomanometer • Airways, oropharyngeal • Syringes • Needles • IV catheters • Antiseptic wipes • Gloves • Sharps disposal box • Urinary catheter • Intravenous fluid system • Venous tourniquet • Sponge gauze • Tape adhesive • Surgical mask • Flashlight and batteries • Thermometer (non-mercury) • Emergency tracheal catheter • Umbilical cord clamp • Basic life support cards • Advance life support cards

Airline terminology

We've explored cabin crew training for safety and security procedures first for obvious reasons followed by first aid for cabin crew. However, a lot of the training is on food service delivery in the cabin; this is an area I'll not go into in much detail as hands-on experience would serve better for this type of learning. Another large section of the training is on aviation jargon so that flight attendants can communicate with colleagues in industry-speak. Air traffic control and pilots are fluent in aviation language, but there are also acronyms that cabin crew need to learn. There are terms for different parts of the aircraft and abbreviations for meals and so forth. There is such a lot to learn, and it's a lot like school, so having a head start is a good move. The next few pages provide a list of just a few abbreviations and the vocabulary that cabin crew need to be familiar with.

Coach – The largest section in the plane for passengers based on class/price of seating, normally referred to as economy.

Concourse/inflight shoes – Female flight attendants wear high heeled shoes at the airport, except when on board the aircraft where they change to flat shoes.

Co-pilot – Also referred to as the First Officer, the person in charge under the Captain.

CSD/CSM – Cabin Service Director or Cabin Service Manager; responsible for the whole team of air cabin crew from the briefing room, during the flight and on the ground at the destination.

EST – Eastern standard time (GMT - 5hrs)

ETA – Estimated time of arrival

First-class – The premium price/zone for passenger service onboard an aircraft.

Flight deck – Also called the cockpit

Galley – This is where meals are prepared and stored along with the beverages.

Jumpseat – The fold-down seat cabin crew use for take-off, landings and during turbulence.

PAX – This refers to the passengers on board. All passengers are listed and special passengers needing assistance are on an additional list.

PDT – Pacific daylight time (GMT - 8hrs)

PIC – Pilot-in-command/Captain

PSU – The passenger service unit is located above each seat and houses the reading light, call button and socket to where oxygen is supplied.

Purser – The supervisor in charge of small teams of cabin crew staff in each section of the aircraft.

Second officer – When there are three personnel in the cockpit, the second officer is the flight engineer.

SEP – Safety and emergency procedures

Widebody Aircraft – This refers to airliners that have more than one aisle in the passenger cabin.

Zulu Time – Universal coordinated time /GMT

Airport codes

Here are some airport codes of meaningful, most enjoyable or favourite destinations that I've travelled to when I was a flight attendant. Find out where they are and add the city and country name next to them.

Airport Code	City	Country
JFK		
LAX		
MIA		
KUL		
DMK		

Now write the airport codes for your favourite destinations. You'd be wise to learn all the airport codes if you want to be in cabin crew.

Africa	Asia	Caribbean	Europe	USA

Carry on with other regions ....

In-flight assessment

Initial job training is half the battle, but the best training is learning on the job where your assessment takes place. In my experience and with many airlines, the purser will monitor and evaluate your performance in service, SEP knowledge, your presentable and polished appearance and your attitude throughout the flight. It can take time to build a portfolio of assessments from different pursers on scheduled trips, but it enables you to earn your wings.

Every airline has its own policy for earning wings, and some external training courses cater for graduates to obtain their wings on course completion. Life is a process of learning, and in this industry, the crew never stop learning. Some companies provide continual professional development (CPD) in a range of courses. During my employment, staff were given the tools to succeed by learning additional and widely spoken languages, SEP refreshers, aircraft models and so on, through what was called The Quest Centre. In your quest to travel, your knowledge will naturally expand as will your learning from experience with passengers.

Fly High

I hope you found these training tips useful and the introductory guidance has given you some direction in what you can expect, what is expected of you and what you can do from now on to learn more and improve your prospects. In hindsight, I would have read loads of manuals and bought or borrowed aviation books before I joined the airline as it gives you confidence during your training and makes the ride a lot smoother. I learnt the hard way, but throughout my training, I was driven by my dream to explore the world and write about my travels. It was my dream and desire to write that was the catalyst for my fly girl life.

At the end of duty on my first working flight, I entered the cockpit (picture above) totally exhausted and technophobic as I was in awe of the control panel. As a child, I loved episodes of *Chips*, an American drama where many scenes showed the cops rescuing civilians in their helicopter, and I dreamed one day that I'd like to do this for an adventure. Today, as someone who enjoys being physically active, I've also wanted to experience piloting a helicopter, even at my age!

It is never too late to have a dream, and your dreams are possible if you are really passionate and want to work hard to pursue them. Regardless of your age, gender, ethnic background or race, if you have a true desire, then fate has a way of showing up for you. People of all ages are now employed as cabin crew, so my final words to you are to Fly High, pursue your dreams, the world is waiting for you!

Acknowledgements

I would like to start by thanking Amanda Epe for gifting me the opportunity to collaborate on this guide. Without her, I would never have had the chance to share my experiences in writing. I would also like to say a big thank you to Patricia Wharton who connected me with Amanda.

A massive thank you to the supporters of #Rash2FlightSchool wherever you may be. Without your support and generosity, I would not be able to complete my flying training and go on to help others achieve their dreams. Last but not least, to my mum for her continued lifelong support.

Rasheed Graham

First, I would like to say it was an honour to work with Rasheed Graham, and I am thankful to Rasheed for collaborating with me. I am also grateful to Patricia Wharton for her community work as presenter Blaze on Chalkhill Community Radio *'The Let's Talk Show where anything can happen'*. That is where this book was conceived as both Rasheed and I were being interviewed.

Thanks to my sister Julie who insists that I keep writing. Finally, thank you to the many children and young people I've worked with who ask, 'Please Miss, can you write some more?'

Amanda Epe

If you are on social media, you can connect

with us at

@rasheedg1_

@flygirlsuk

Or if you found our work useful, please leave

a review on Amazon.